M000198809

WHAT THE BIBLE SAYS ABOUT

Forgiveness

ROSE PUBLISHING

Torrance, California

What the Bible Says About Forgiveness
© 2015 Bristol Works, Inc.

Rose Publishing, Inc.
4733 Torrance Blvd., #259
Torrance, California 90503 USA
www.rose-publishing.com

Printed in the United States of America
010915RRD

Contents

Forgiveness Is Needed

"Forgive us our sins, for we also forgive everyone who sins against us." —Luke 11:4

With these familiar words in the Lord's Prayer, we are reminded that forgiveness should characterize our lives. But these few words are perhaps a lot easier said than done. Forgiveness is one of the hardest things to do because the sins that need forgiving can be so damaging. People have wounded us so deeply that the mere idea of offering forgiveness to those who hurt us seems impossible.

Forgiveness, in these cases, appears like letting people off the hook for their transgressions. The sharp pain in our hearts creates a barrier that prevents us from moving beyond our pain. Our pain and brokenness seem unending.

In the face of so much brokenness in ourselves and in our world, how should we respond? Should we deny it? Ignore it? Get even? Give up? God's Word says to forgive it. Forgiveness will never be easy. However, only through forgiveness can healing begin.

Most of us can relate to many kinds of brokenness. Here are a few examples of situations in which forgiveness might be very difficult.

Emotional

- Abandonment by a father or mother

- Infidelity, divorce, lying

- Betrayal by a trusted friend or confidant

Physical

- Sexual or domestic abuse

- Parental neglect of a child's physical needs

- Assault or violence

Spiritual

- Misuse of authority by a church leader

- Rejection or poor treatment by a church "family"

- Major sins committed by a pastor

- Private sins that damage a person's relationship with God

Financial

- Stealing, embezzlement, fraud

- Failure to repay a debt or loan

- Unfair loss of a job or employment discrimination

Social

- Name calling, insults, public humiliation

- Loss of reputation from gossip and lies

- Discrimination from prejudices, racism, or sexism

- Bullying, cyber-bullying

Forgiveness exists because sin exists. Forgiveness is necessary because sin powerfully affects all areas of our lives. Forgiveness is not about ignoring evil, excusing it, or making light of it. On the contrary, forgiveness courageously faces sin and evil. Forgiveness acknowledges that a terrible wrong has been done and seeks to do something about it.

SIN IS REAL

No one needs to look far to see that there is sin in the world. We are born into a world where harmful patterns of sin persist in societies, communities, churches, and families. We may not even be aware of our own contribution to the cycles of sin. Because sin is in the world and in us, we need forgiveness even more.

> *If we claim to be without sin, we deceive ourselves and the truth is not in us. If we confess our sins, he is faithful and just and will forgive us our sins and purify us from all unrighteousness. If we claim we have not sinned, we make him out to be a liar and his word is not in us.* —1 John 1:8–10

"One great power of sin is that it blinds men so that they do not recognize its true character."

—Andrew Murray,
19th-century South
African pastor

SIN IS DESTRUCTIVE

Sin breaks our communion with God and destroys our relationships with others. The first human sin brought death into the world for all to suffer the consequences. When someone hurts us, our pain and our sin begin a cycle of anger, violence, resentment, and revenge that increases over time. Only forgiveness can allow us to break this cycle.

> *Therefore, just as sin entered the world through one man, and death through sin, and in this way death came to all people, because all sinned.* —Romans 5:12

> *Once you were alienated from God and were enemies in your minds because of your evil behavior.* —Colossians 1:21

What causes fights and quarrels among you? Don't they come from your desires that battle within you? You desire but do not have, so you kill. You covet, but you cannot get what you want, so you quarrel and fight.
—James 4:1–2a

GOD TAKES SIN SERIOUSLY

Scripture tells us that God is merciful and forgiving, but it also makes clear that God does not tolerate sin. Because sin is so harmful, it demands divine judgment, not mere dismissal.

And he passed in front of Moses, proclaiming, "The LORD, the LORD, the compassionate and gracious God, slow to anger, abounding in love and faithfulness, maintaining love to thousands, and forgiving wickedness, rebellion and sin. Yet he does not leave the guilty unpunished; he punishes the children and their children for the sin of the parents to the third and fourth generation."
—Exodus 34:6–7

The acts of the flesh are obvious: sexual immorality, impurity and debauchery; idolatry and witchcraft; hatred, discord, jealousy, fits of rage, selfish ambition, dissensions, factions and envy; drunkenness, orgies, and the like. I warn you, as I did before, that those who live like this will not inherit the kingdom of God. —Galatians 5:19–20

For the wages of sin is death, but the gift of God is eternal life in Christ Jesus our Lord.
—Romans 6:23

"Forgiveness is God's invention for coming to terms with a world in which, despite their best intentions, people are unfair to each other and hurt each other deeply. He began by forgiving us. And he invites us all to forgive each other."

—Lewis B. Smedes

Forgiveness Is Possible

If judgment of sin were the last word on the matter, we would all stay trapped in our guilt and brokenness. If vengeance for every offense were the only option, we would forever remain separated from our Creator. But thank God he has provided another way—the way of forgiveness. Forgiveness does not erase the past, but it gives us a chance for a better future.

GOD DESIRES TO FORGIVE

The Old Testament contains many examples of God sending punishment for sinful acts. However, his withholding of judgment was for the purpose of bringing the people back to God so he could forgive them and restore the broken relationship. Though our actions deserve judgment, God desires to be merciful.

If my people, who are called by my name, will humble themselves and pray and seek my face and turn from their wicked ways, then I will hear from heaven and I will forgive their sin and will heal their land. —2 Chronicles 7:14

Perhaps when the people of Judah hear about every disaster I plan to inflict on them, they will turn from their wicked ways; then I will forgive their wickedness and their sin. —Jeremiah 36:3

The LORD is compassionate and gracious, slow to anger, abounding in love. He will not always accuse, nor will he harbor his anger forever; he does not treat us as our sins deserve or repay us according to our iniquities. For as high as the heavens are above the earth, so great is his love for those who fear him; as far as the east is from the west, so far has he removed our transgressions from us.
—Psalm 103:8–12

JESUS MADE FORGIVENESS POSSIBLE

In the New Testament, we see God's desire to forgive expressed most clearly in the life and death of his Son. Jesus' sinless life and voluntary death atoned for the world's sins. He bore the ultimate judgment of sin so we don't have to. God forgives us because he loves us.

In him we have redemption through his blood, the forgiveness of sins, in accordance with the riches of God's grace.
—Ephesians 1:7

For he has rescued us from the dominion of darkness and brought us into the kingdom of the Son he loves, in whom we have redemption, the forgiveness of sins. —Colossians 1:13–14

Therefore, my friends, I want you to know that through Jesus the forgiveness of sins is proclaimed to you. —Acts 13:38

But God demonstrates his own love for us in this: While we were still sinners, Christ died for us.
—Romans 5:8

FORGIVENESS IS AVAILABLE

When we place our faith in Jesus, we are declared free from divine condemnation and we stand forgiven of our sin. Forgiveness, not judgment, is the final word.

> *Therefore, there is now no condemnation for those who are in Christ Jesus, because through Christ Jesus the law of the Spirit of life has set you free from the law of sin and death.* —Romans 8:1–2

> *Peter replied, "Repent and be baptized, every one of you, in the name of Jesus Christ for the forgiveness of your sins. And you will receive the gift of the Holy Spirit."* —Acts 2:38

I, even I, am he who blots out your transgressions, for my own sake, and remembers your sins no more. —Isaiah 43:25

All the prophets testify about him that everyone who believes in him receives forgiveness of sins through his name. —Acts 10:43

"Forgiving love is a possibility only for those who know that they are not good, who feel themselves in need of divine mercy ... [who] feel themselves as well as their fellow men convicted of sin by a holy God and know that the differences between the good man and the bad man are insignificant in his sight."

—Reinhold Niebuhr

Forgiveness Is Ongoing

Forgiveness is not a one-time thing. We need to continue to ask God for forgiveness for the wrongs we commit even after our initial acceptance of Jesus. In response to such generous forgiveness, God entrusts us with the responsibility and privilege to mirror his love by forgiving those who sin against us.

ASK FOR FORGIVENESS AS OFTEN AS NEEDED

As believers, we are made right with God through Jesus, yet old patterns of sin may still resurface. Sinful habits in our lives hurt others and impede a growing, vibrant relationship with God. We continue to be in need of God's forgiveness daily, and are instructed to ask forgiveness from anyone whom we have wronged.

> *My dear children, I write this to you so that you will not sin. But if anybody does sin, we have one who speaks to the Father in our defense—Jesus Christ, the Righteous One. He is the atoning sacrifice for our sins, and not only for ours but also for the sins of the whole world.* —1 John 2:1–2

Therefore, if you are offering your gift at the altar and there remember that your brother or sister has something against you, leave your gift there in front of the altar. First go and be reconciled to them; then come and offer your gift. —Matthew 5:23–24

Therefore confess your sins to each other and pray for each other so that you may be healed. —James 5:16

FORGIVE OTHERS AS OFTEN AS NEEDED

God forgives us time and time again, and he calls us to do the same. There is no limit to how often or how many times we are to forgive others. God wants his forgiven people to be forgivers.

> *If your brother or sister sins against you, rebuke them, and if they repent, forgive them. Even if they sin against you seven times in a day, and seven times come back to you saying "I repent," you must forgive them.* —Luke 17:3–4

> *Bear with each other and forgive one another if any of you has a grievance against someone. Forgive as the Lord forgave you. And over all these virtues put on love, which binds them all together in perfect unity.*
> —Colossians 3:13–14

Why Forgive

FORGIVENESS FREES THE FORGIVER

Anyone who has been wronged knows that forgiveness is not easy. However, resentment and bitterness are damaging. If anger is allowed to fester it will spill over into other areas of life, destroying relationships and leading to a path of revenge.

Make every effort to live in peace with everyone and to be holy; without holiness no one will see the Lord. See to it that no one falls

*short of the grace of God and that
no bitter root grows up to cause
trouble and defile many.*
—Hebrews 12:14–15

*Finally, all of you, be like-minded,
be sympathetic, love one another,
be compassionate and humble.
Do not repay evil with evil or
insult with insult. On the contrary,
repay evil with blessing, because
to this you were called so that
you may inherit a blessing.*
—1 Peter 3:8–9

"Resentment is like a glass of poison that a man drinks; then he sits down and waits for his enemy to die."

—Author Unknown

FORGIVE SO THAT YOU WILL BE FORGIVEN

If we want to be forgiven ourselves, we must extend that same forgiveness to others, allowing forgiveness to triumph over the desire to extract retribution.

> *"For if you forgive other people when they sin against you, your heavenly Father will also forgive you. But if you do not forgive others their sins, your Father will not forgive your sins."*
> —Matthew 6:14–15

> *Speak and act as those who are going to be judged by the law that gives freedom, because judgment without mercy will be shown to anyone who has not been merciful. Mercy triumphs over judgment.* —James 2:12–13

"And when you stand praying, if you hold anything against anyone, forgive them, so that your Father in heaven may forgive you your sins." —Mark 11:25

"Do not judge, and you will not be judged. Do not condemn, and you will not be condemned. Forgive, and you will be forgiven." —Luke 6:37

"Without forgiveness, there's no future."

—Desmond Tutu,
Anglican Archbishop
who opposed apartheid
(racial segregation) in
South Africa

HEALING RELATIONSHIPS REQUIRES FORGIVENESS

Often the key to healing relationships begins with forgiveness. God is working in the world to reconcile fallen humans to himself through Christ, and he calls us to be ministers of reconciliation in this broken world.

> *Once you were alienated from God and were enemies in your minds because of your evil behavior. But now he has reconciled you by Christ's physical body through death to present you holy in his sight, without blemish and free from accusation—if you continue in your faith, established and firm, and do not move from the hope held out in the gospel.*
> —Colossians 1:21–23

All this is from God, who reconciled us to himself through Christ and gave us the ministry of reconciliation: that God was reconciling the world to himself in Christ, not counting people's sins against them. And he has committed to us the message of reconciliation. We are therefore Christ's ambassadors, as though God were making his appeal through us. We implore you on Christ's behalf: Be reconciled to God. —2 Corinthians 5:18–20
(See also Romans 5:6–11)

If anyone has caused grief, he has not so much grieved me as he has grieved all of you, to some extent—not to put it too severely. The punishment inflicted on him by the majority is sufficient. Now instead, you ought to forgive and comfort him, so that he will not be overwhelmed by excessive sorrow. I urge you, therefore, to reaffirm your love for him.

—2 Corinthians 2:5–8

FORGIVENESS IS A TESTIMONY OF GOD'S LOVE

The world tells us to "get even" or "make them sorry!" God says something quite different. God's love for all people motivates us to love others as well— even the most unlovable! When we forgive, we demonstrate God's love for a sinful world.

> *"But I tell you: Love your enemies and pray for those who persecute you, that you may be children of your Father in heaven. He causes his sun to rise on the evil and the good, and sends rain on the righteous and the unrighteous. If you love those who love you, what reward will you get? Are not even the tax collectors doing that? And if you greet only your own people, what are you doing more*

than others? Do not even pagans do that? Be perfect, therefore, as your heavenly Father is perfect."
—Matthew 5:44–48

"We forgive with no strings attached; that may require us to forgive repeatedly. When we do, we shock the world with God's power at work within us."

— Rebecca Nichols Alonzo,
who, at age seven, witnessed
her mother's murder

DOES FORGIVENESS MEAN RECONCILIATION?

A common reason people withhold forgiveness is that they think that forgiveness requires immediate and total reconciliation with the offender. People who have been hurt ask: If I forgive, does that mean I have to put myself back in the abusive situation? Must I force myself to be best friends again with the person who wronged me? Am I required to give the betrayer my full trust?

No, forgiveness is not the same as reconciliation. Forgiveness involves letting go of vengeance and hatred for being wronged. Reconciliation can be described as "restoration to harmony in relationship." One person can forgive, but it takes two people to restore a broken relationship. Forgiveness alone neither guarantees nor demands reconciliation. Often much more is needed before reconciliation can (or should) take place, for example: repentance, restitution of the wrong, gaining back trust, or evidence of genuine change. If forgiveness is taken to mean "going back" to the offender as if nothing ever happened, then people will end up only with a cheap imitation of reconciliation, far unlike the genuine harmony in a restored relationship described in Scripture.

Therefore encourage one another and build each other up, just as in fact you are doing.
—1 Thessalonians 5:11

Love must be sincere. Hate what is evil; cling to what is good. Be devoted to one another in love. Honor one another above yourselves. Never be lacking in zeal, but keep your spiritual fervor, serving the Lord. Be joyful in hope, patient in affliction, faithful in prayer. Share with the Lord's people who are in need. Practice hospitality. Bless those who persecute you; bless and do not curse. Rejoice with those who rejoice; mourn with those who mourn. Live in harmony with one another. Do not be proud, but be willing to associate with people of low position. Do not be conceited. —Romans 12:9–16

*"Forgiveness is unlocking
the door to set someone free
and realizing you were
the prisoner!"*

—Author Unknown

How to Forgive

PRACTICE FORGIVENESS BEFORE IT'S NEEDED

A runner who finishes a marathon has gotten into the habit of running, long before the start of the race. In the same way, if we want to be able to forgive the big stuff, we have to get into the habit of forgiving the small stuff. Forgiveness, like other virtues, takes daily cultivation.

Above all, love each other deeply, because love covers over a multitude of sins. —1 Peter 4:8

Get rid of all bitterness, rage and anger, brawling and slander, along with every form of malice. Be kind and compassionate to one another, forgiving each other, just as in Christ God forgave you.
—Ephesians 4:31–32

EXAMINE YOUR OWN SIN

Recognizing our own need for God's forgiveness enables us to see our offender's need for mercy. The practice of the Lord's Supper (Communion) reminds us that we are all flawed and sinful people in need of forgiveness. Self-righteousness will breed an unforgiving heart, but through humility we can learn to extend mercy to others.

He who conceals their sins does not prosper, but the one who confesses and renounces them finds mercy. —Proverbs 28:13

But who can discern their own errors? Forgive my hidden faults.
—Psalm 19:12

Then he took the cup, gave thanks and offered it to them, saying, "Drink from it, all of you. This is my blood of the covenant, which is poured out for many for the forgiveness of sins."
—Matthew 26:27–28

"That is the whole lesson: the sins of others you see, but your own sin you fail to see. In repentance, recognize God's mercy toward you: in this way alone will you be able to forgive."

— Dietrich Bonhoeffer, German pastor and theologian who was imprisoned and executed for his opposition to Nazism

GIVE UP YOUR RIGHT TO REVENGE

Anger is a natural response when we are harmed. But God's Word says to be careful that our anger does not result in taking revenge. We should not add sin upon sin, but leave the situation where it belongs—in God's hands. (See also 1 Thessalonians 5:15.)

> *Do not say, "I'll pay you back for this wrong!" Wait for the LORD, and he will avenge you.*
> —Proverbs 20:22

> *In your anger do not sin: Do not let the sun go down while you are still angry, and do not give the devil a foothold.*
> —Ephesians 4:26–27

Bless those who persecute you;
bless and do not curse. ...
Do not repay anyone evil for evil.
Be careful to do what is right
in the eyes of everyone. If it is
possible, as far as it depends on
you, live at peace with everyone.
Do not take revenge, my friends,
but leave room for God's wrath,
for it is written: "It is mine to
avenge; I will repay," says the
Lord. On the contrary: "If your
enemy is hungry, feed him; if
he is thirsty, give him something
to drink. In doing this, you will
heap burning coals on his head."
Do not be overcome by evil, but
overcome evil with good.

—Romans 12:14, 17–21

LEARN FROM VETERAN FORGIVERS

There is no cookie-cutter way to forgive. Every situation is different. For instance, how to go about forgiving a close friend who has betrayed you will be different from how to forgive an unknown hit-and-run driver. We can gain wisdom in knowing how to deal with particular situations by taking note of Christians who have already walked the path of forgiveness. Their examples and guidance can give us a long-term view beyond the initial feelings of anger and pain.

> *Join together in following my example, brothers and sisters, and just as you have us as a model, keep your eyes on those who live as we do.* —Philippians 3:17

Brothers and sisters, as an example of patience in the face of suffering, take the prophets who spoke in the name of the Lord. As you know, we consider blessed those who have persevered. You have heard of Job's perseverance and have seen what the Lord finally brought about. The Lord is full of compassion and mercy.
—James 5:10–11

LET FORGIVENESS TAKE TIME

The apostle Paul compares the Christian life to a race that we have not yet finished. This side of heaven we may not be able to forgive to the extent that we want to because we are still imperfect people in an imperfect world. What we are called to do is to continue moving forward and not to give up.

> *Not that I have already obtained all this, or have already arrived at my goal, but I press on to take hold of that for which Christ Jesus took hold of me. Brothers and sisters, I do not consider myself yet to have taken hold of it. But one thing I do: Forgetting what is behind and straining toward what is ahead, I press on toward the goal to win the prize for which God has called me heavenward in Christ Jesus. All of us who are*

mature should take such a view of things. And if on some point you think differently, that too God will make clear to you. Only let us live up to what we have already attained. —Philippians 3:12–16

"Forgiveness stretches out over time, but you have to start out with the will to forgive. But the bitterness may reenter your mind from time to time, and then you have to think about forgiveness again."

— An Amish mother whose daughter was killed when a gunman opened fire in a schoolhouse

PRAY FOR YOUR ENEMIES

It might sound cliché to say "just pray about it," but there is nothing trite about praying for someone who has wronged you. Such prayers can have a powerful effect on the person praying. By the power of God's Spirit in us, through prayer, God can miraculously change our hatred into love.

> *"But I tell you: Love your enemies and pray for those who persecute you, that you may be children of your Father in heaven."*
> —Matthew 5:44–45

> *In the same way, the Spirit helps us in our weakness. We do not know what we ought to pray for, but the Spirit himself intercedes for us through wordless groans.*
> —Romans 8:26

But [the Lord] said to me, "My grace is sufficient for you, for my power is made perfect in weakness." ... For when I am weak, then I am strong.

—2 Corinthians 12:9–10

TRUST IN GOD'S GOODNESS

Placing a painful situation in God's hands is only possible if we allow ourselves to trust that God knows best. When we give it over to God, we will be surprised at the good he will bring out of any bad situation. The best example of God's goodness transcending evil is that of Jesus' death on the cross. What appeared to many to be the pointless crucifixion of an innocent man turned out to be the means whereby God provided forgiveness of sins for the world. Jesus trusted the Father that the way of forgiveness would be the best path.

> *To this you were called, because Christ suffered for you, leaving you an example, that you should follow in his steps. "He committed no sin, and no deceit was found in his mouth." When*

they hurled their insults at him, he did not retaliate; when he suffered, he made no threats. Instead, he entrusted himself to him who judges justly. "He himself bore our sins" in his body on the cross, so that we might die to sins and live for righteousness; "by his wounds you have been healed." —1 Peter 2:21–24

Loving your "enemies" is to see them as fellow human beings who are loved by God and in need of his grace; but it is not to tolerate their abuse or invite them to hurt you again. The so-called "love" that ignores or allows such damaging sins is not really love at all.

"When we are powerless to do a thing, it is a great joy that we can come and step inside the ability of Jesus."

— Corrie ten Boom,
  Holocaust survivor

DEALING WITH ANGER

Sometimes anger and bitterness prevent us from experiencing the freedom of forgiveness. The following steps can help us break free from the chains of anger.

1. *Acknowledge God's complete forgiveness by grace.*

I am forgiven by the grace of God!

For he has rescued us from the dominion of darkness and brought us into the kingdom of the Son he loves, in whom we have redemption, the forgiveness of sins. —Colossians 1:3–14

2. *Be willing to confess your bitterness and resentment to God.*

God, forgive my bitter attitudes and my anger toward _____.

Create in me a pure heart, O God, and renew a steadfast spirit within me. Do not cast me from your presence or take your Holy Spirit from me. Restore to me the joy of your salvation and grant me a willing spirit, to sustain me.
—Psalm 51:10–12

3. Recognize that your anger is a violation of God's Word and choose to release the anger.

With the Holy Spirit's help, I choose to lay down this anger. I release my desire for revenge on _____.

Make every effort to live in peace with everyone and to be holy; without holiness no one will see the Lord. See to it that no one falls short of the grace of God and that no bitter root grows up to cause trouble and defile many.
—Hebrews 12:14–15

4. Follow the Holy Spirit's leading as to whether you need to speak to the person you need to forgive.

God, I ask for your Spirit to guide me into what I should do next.

Speak and act as those who are going to be judged by the law that gives freedom, because judgment without mercy will be shown to anyone who has not been merciful. Mercy triumphs over judgment. —James 2:12–13

Go through these steps repeatedly until words become experience.

WHEN WE REFUSE TO FORGIVE

Forgiveness is characteristic of a Christian life. By loving our enemies, we show that we are children of God. When a Christian refuses to forgive, that person puts himself above God as judge.

> *"Blessed are the merciful, for they will be shown mercy."*
> —Matthew 5:7

> *"You have heard that it was said, 'Love your neighbor and hate your enemy.' But I tell you: Love your enemies and pray for those who persecute you, that you may be sons of your Father in heaven. He causes his sun to rise on the evil and the good, and sends rain on the righteous and the unrighteous."* —Matthew 5:43–45

WHEN WE CHOOSE TO FORGIVE

We follow Jesus, our role model, who forgave. We are made in the image of God, who forgives.

Forgiveness keeps Satan from gaining a foothold. Christ's Body, the Church, cannot function without forgiveness. Only by forgiving others can we expect our own prayers for forgiveness to be answered. Only through Jesus are we forgiven and made right with God. Whatever we may suffer cannot come close to the offenses Jesus Christ forgave during his time on earth.

"To be a Christian means
to forgive the inexcusable
because God has forgiven
the inexcusable in you."

—C. S. Lewis

We reflect the beauty and glory of our Creator when we forgive. Forgiveness frees the conscience of guilt and brings peace of mind. Grudges and resentments tarnish the Church's witness and prevent the full benefits of God's gifts.

LOVE KEEPS NO RECORD OF WRONGS

In one of the most beloved passages of Scripture, 1 Corinthians 13, the apostle Paul explains what love is and what it is not.

> *Love is patient, love is kind. It does not envy, it does not boast, it is not proud. It does not dishonor others, it is not self-seeking, it is not easily angered, it **keeps no record of wrongs**. Love does not delight in evil but rejoices with the truth. It always protects, always trusts, always hopes, always perseveres.*
> —1 Corinthians 13:4–7 (emphasis added)

Keeping a record wrongs may mean:

- Not letting go of past injustices until bitterness takes root in your heart.

- Literally keeping a long list of all the ways people have let you down and hurt you.

- Planning revenge on those who have done wrong.

- Reminding others of how they have failed you in the past—and probably will in the future.

Keeping a record of wrong is the opposite of being kind and forgiving.

The Bible says …

> Do not say, "I'll do to them as they have done to me; I'll pay them back for what they did."
> —Proverbs 24:29

When we do not forgive, we keep a detailed track of all the offenses others has done against us. Keeping a record of wrongs leads to grudges and inner bitterness. A disgruntled heart can turn into a heart that plans evil against the other. When people reach this point, relationships are truly in danger of perishing. Forgiveness is critical.

But forgiveness—genuine forgiveness— is not putting on a face. Pretending everything is okay only causes hidden resentment. It may seem easier to avoid conflict, to retreat and hide, and pretend things are well. Until we have dealt with the deep things of the heart, we will not have forgiven.

WHY WE CAN LET GO

Jesus took God's true record of our wrongs and nailed it to the cross. He paid the price for us. We do not have to hold on to bitterness, resentment, or unforgiveness.

> *When you were dead in your sins and in the uncircumcision of your flesh, God made you alive with Christ. He forgave us all our sins, having canceled the charge of our legal indebtedness, which stood against us and condemned us; he has taken it away, nailing it to the cross.* —Colossians 2:13–14

Stories of Forgiveness in the Bible

JACOB AND ESAU

Genesis 25:19–34; 27:1–28:9;
32:1–21; 33

Brokenness

From their birth, the brothers Jacob and
Esau were rivals. Jacob, the younger
brother, went so far as to deceive
their aged father into giving him Esau's
blessing. Esau was so furious that he
vowed to kill his brother.

Forgiveness
After years of estrangement, Esau forgave Jacob and the brothers were reconciled.

Key Verse
But Esau ran to meet Jacob and embraced him; he threw his arms around his neck and kissed him. And they wept. —Genesis 33:4

JOSEPH AND HIS BROTHERS
Genesis 37–50

Brokenness
Joseph's brothers were jealous that Joseph, the youngest, was favored by their father. The brothers sold Joseph to slave traders who took him to Egypt. When Joseph rose to a place of power in Egypt he had the choice to punish his brothers or forgive them and provide food for them through a severe famine.

Forgiveness
Joseph chose to forgive his brothers and provide for their needs.

Key Verse
Joseph said: "You intended to harm me, but God intended it for good to accomplish what is now being done, the saving of many lives."
—Genesis 50:20

DAVID AND GOD
2 Samuel 11:1–12:25; Psalm 51

Brokenness

David took Bathsheba, the wife of one of his loyal soldiers. When Bathsheba became pregnant, David tried many ways to hide his sin—even making sure that her husband was killed on the battlefield! But David couldn't hide his sin from God. God sent the prophet Nathan to confront David about the evil he had done.

> *Then David confessed to Nathan, "I have sinned against the LORD." Nathan replied, "Yes, but the Lord has forgiven you, and you won't die for this sin. Nevertheless, because you have shown utter contempt for the word of the Lord by doing this, your child will die."*
> —2 Samuel 12:13–14, NLT

Forgiveness
David cried out to God for forgiveness. God forgave him, but the child David and Bathsheba had did not live.

Key Verse
Wash away all my iniquity and cleanse me from my sin. For I know my transgressions, and my sin is always before me. —Psalm 51:2–3

JESUS AND A FORGIVEN WOMAN
Luke 7:36–50

Brokenness
A woman, who is described in Scripture as living "a sinful life," came to Jesus weeping. She anointed his feet in a public display of adoration.

Forgiveness
Because she was forgiven much she loved Jesus much.

Key Verse
Jesus said: "Therefore, I tell you, her many sins have been forgiven—as her great love has shown. But whoever has been forgiven little loves little."
—Luke 7:47

A FATHER AND HIS REBELLIOUS SON
Luke 15:11–32

Brokenness
Jesus told a parable about a son who asked for his inheritance while his father was still living. The son left his father and squandered his inheritance on a sinful lifestyle. When the son was finally at the lowest point of his life, he decided to return his father to confess his sin and ask his father to take him back merely as a servant in his household.

Forgiveness
The father goes far beyond what his son had hoped, and he welcomed him back into his household with celebration, still as a beloved son.

Key Verse

But while [the son] was still a long way off, his father saw him and was filled with compassion for him; he ran to his son, threw his arms around him and kissed him. —Luke 15:20

©Nancy Bauer / Shutterstock.com

A MAN WHO BEGGED FOR MERCY
Luke 18:9–14

Brokenness
Jesus told a parable of two men who went to the temple to pray. One man, a teacher of religious law, thanked God that he was not like people who need forgiveness. The other man, a tax collector (a profession known at that time for cheating people and enforcing unjust laws), begged God for mercy.

Forgiveness
The tax collector went home justified before God because he recognized that he was a sinner, while the religious teacher did not because he failed to see his own need for forgiveness.

Key Verse

But the tax collector stood at a distance. He would not even look up to heaven, but beat his breast and said, "God, have mercy on me, a sinner." —Luke 18:13

JESUS AND A WOMAN CAUGHT IN ADULTERY
John 8:1–11

Brokenness
The religious leaders tried to use a woman who had been caught in adultery to trap Jesus. They brought her before Jesus and asked if she should be stoned to death for her sin.

Forgiveness
Instead of answering immediately, Jesus began to write on the ground. Then he said to them, "Let any one of you who is without sin be the first to throw a stone at her." One by one, her accusers left in shame.

Key Verse
"Then neither do I condemn you,"
Jesus declared. "Go now and leave
your life of sin." —John 8:11

JESUS AND THOSE WHO CRUCIFIED HIM

Luke 23:32–43

Brokenness

Jesus was falsely accused, sent to his death by an angry crowd and corrupt leaders, and executed on the cross by Roman soldiers.

Forgiveness

Jesus asked the Father to forgive those who crucified him.

Key Verse

"Father, forgive them, for they do not know what they are doing."
—Luke 23:34

PETER AND JESUS
John 13:31–38; 18:15–27; 21:15–19

Brokenness
Jesus' disciple, Peter, professed that he would go so far as to lay down his life for Jesus. But when Jesus was arrested, Peter ended up denying three times that he was even a follower of Jesus.

Forgiveness
After Jesus' resurrection, he gave Peter the opportunity to restate his devotion to Jesus three times—which Peter did. Jesus restored Peter to a place of importance among the disciples.

Key Verse
Jesus asked [Peter] the third time, "Do you love me?" He said, "Lord, you know all things; you know that I love you." Jesus said, "Feed my sheep."
—John 21:17

STEPHEN AND THOSE
WHO KILLED HIM
Acts 7:54–60

Brokenness
Stephen, a believer in Jesus, boldly proclaimed the gospel of Christ. An infuriated crowed who didn't want to hear what Stephen said picked up stones and killed him in public.

Forgiveness
As Stephen was dying, he asked God to forgive those who were stoning him.

Key Verse
He fell to his knees, shouting, "Lord, don't charge them with this sin!" And with that, he died. —Acts 7:60 NLT

THE PARABLE OF THE UNMERCIFUL SERVANT
Matthew 18:21–35

Peter's Question:

> *"Lord, how many times shall I forgive my brother or sister who sins against me? Up to seven times?"* —Matthew 18:21

Peter probably thought his "seven times" suggestion was generous since the rabbis of the day taught that one should forgive only up to three times.

Jesus' Answer:

> *"No, not seven times," Jesus replied, "but seventy times seven!"* —Matthew 18:22 NLT

If Peter was fishing for a cap on forgiveness, Jesus gave him an impossible limit, which was really no limit at all. Jesus explained why we should forgive with a story about a king and a servant who owes the king a lot of money.

The Merciful King:

Is owed a massive debt of 10,000 bags of gold (v. 24). This is a way of saying it is an incalculable sum, like saying "billions of dollars."

The Unmerciful Servant:

Is owed a small debt (v. 28). The debt the servant owes the king is about 600,000 times more than what the servant is owed by a fellow servant.

The Merciful King:

Is moved to compassion by the servant's plea in which the servant promises to pay a debt which is clearly impossible for him to do (v. 26).

The Unmerciful Servant:

Becomes violent and chokes the servant who owes him, and refuses to listen when the servant pleads for mercy (v. 29).

The Merciful King:

Cancels the entire debt and lets the servant walk away a debt-free man instead of being sold into slavery as the law allowed (v. 27).

The Unmerciful Servant:

Throws his fellow servant into a debtor's prison (v. 30).

When the unmerciful servant's actions are exposed:

- The fellow servants are outraged and report his conduct to the king (v. 31).

- This time the king is moved to anger, not compassion (v. 34).

- The servant is called "wicked" by the king (v. 32).

- The king renews the debt and hands the servant over to jailers (v. 34).

The Lesson

> *"This is how my heavenly Father will treat each of you unless you forgive your brother or sister from your heart."* —Matthew 18:35

Our debt to God is enormous, and his forgiveness is extravagant. In light of this, Jesus allows no excuse for withholding forgiveness from others.

"God's forgiveness is unconditional: it comes from a heart that does not demand anything for itself, a heart that is completely empty of self-seeking. It is this divine forgiveness that I have to practice in my daily life. It calls me to keep stepping over all my arguments that say forgiveness is unwise, unhealthy, and impractical.

It challenges me to step over all my needs for gratitude and compliments. Finally, it demands of me that I step over that wounded part of my heart that feels hurt and wronged and that wants to stay in control and put a few conditions between me and the one whom I am asked to forgive."

—Henri Nouwen

OTHER GREAT STORIES OF FORGIVENESS

The Devil in Pew Number Seven by Rebecca Nichols Alonzo (Tyndale House, 2010)

> The true story of a young girl who, at age seven, witnessed her mother's murder.

No Future Without Forgiveness by Desmond Tutu (Random House, 2000)

> Desmond Tutu is an Anglican Bishop and Nobel Peace Prize winner known for his relentless opposition to apartheid (racial segregation) in South Africa in the 1980s.

The Hiding Place by Corrie ten Boom
(Random House, 1982)

> The story of Holocaust survivor
> Corrie ten Boom who was sent to
> a concentration camp for helping
> Jews escape the Nazis.

*Bonhoeffer: Pastor, Martyr, Prophet,
Spy* by Eric Metaxas (Thomas Nelson,
2010)

> A biography of German pastor
> Dietrich Bonhoeffer who was
> imprisoned and executed for
> participating in a covert movement
> to resist the Nazis.

In the Presence of My Enemies by
Gracia Burnham (Tyndale, 2003, 2009)

> The story of missionaries Martin
> and Gracia Burnham who were
> kidnapped by a terrorist group in
> the Philippines.

Amish Grace: How Forgiveness Transcended Tragedy by Donald B. Kraybill, Steven M. Nolt, and David L. Weaver-Zercher (Jossey Bass, 2007)

> How an Amish community in Pennsylvania grappled with the tragedy of a gunman who walked into a schoolhouse and killed five children.

Forgive and Forget: Healing the Hurts We Don't Deserve 2nd ed. by Lewis B. Smedes (HarperOne, 2007); *The Art of Forgiving: When You Need to Forgive and Don't Know How* by Lewis B. Smedes (Ballantine Books, 1996)

> Practical advice about how to forgive those who have hurt you deeply.

You Might Also Like

What the Bible Says about Prayer
ISBN: 9781628622027

What the Bible Says about Forgiveness
ISBN: 9781628622034

What the Bible Says about Money
ISBN: 9781628622041

Following Jesus
ISBN: 9781628622058

Names of God
ISBN: 9781628620863

How to Study the Bible
ISBN: 9781628620856

Book of Psalms
ISBN: 9781628620832

The Love Chapter
ISBN: 9781628620849